In the Fields

By Michele Spirn
Illustrated by Carlotta Tormey

Scott Foresman
is an imprint of

PEARSON

Glenview, Illinois • Boston, Massachusetts • Chandler, Arizona •
Upper Saddle River, New Jersey

Illustrations
Carlotta A. Tormey.

Photographs
Every effort has been made to secure permission and provide appropriate credit for photographic material. The publisher deeply regrets any omission and pledges to correct errors called to its attention in subsequent editions.

Unless otherwise acknowledged, all photographs are the property of Pearson Education, Inc.

16 Arthur Schatz/Time Life Pictures/Getty Images.

ISBN 13: 978-0-328-51384-0
ISBN 10:   0-328-51384-9

7 8 9 10 V0FL 16 15 14 13

"I'm so thirsty," said Luis. He picked the bunches of grapes from the grapevines slowly and placed them in the tray below him.

"I'm sorry, son," said his father, Tomas. "The water in the fields in this area of California is not safe to drink. You'll have to wait until we finish today to get a drink."

"Why can't we work someplace where there's clean water?" Luis asked.

"We're lucky to have this job," Luis's mother said. "Now be quiet and work."

Luis knew his mother and father were worried about making enough money to last through the winter. It would be hard to find jobs in the winter.

He looked at the shack they were now living in while they worked in these fields. It was hot because of the tin roof. The water they had carried this morning from the well a mile away was hot too. There was no refrigerator to keep things cold. His mother had tried to make the shack seem like home. Even with his mother's bunch of bright red artificial flowers, this wasn't the home that Luis dreamed of having.

The next day, some men came by the field
to sort what Luis had picked. Luis knew that
some of the grapes would be made into raisins.
To make raisins, the grapes would be dried
in the sun on paper trays. Luis knew it took
about three weeks for the grapes to dry. Then
a preservative would be added to keep them
fresh so that they would last for a long time.

One of the younger men took his father aside. As he picked his grapes, Luis could hear them talking nearby.

"So, Tomas, are you ready to join us?" he heard the man ask.

"It's a lot to ask, Tonio," said his father. "I have a family to support."

"Do you want your son and daughter growing up to pick under these conditions?" the younger man, Tonio, asked. "No clean water. Bad places to live. This is 1965. No one should have to work and live like this."

"I'll think about it," his father promised, "but I have to have some proof that this is going to work."

"I can't promise that it will," Tonio said, "but we must try. You should join us. We're going to raise a group of grape pickers so big that no one can ignore us."

That night, Luis wanted to know about the man in the field. "What was that man talking about today, Papa?" he said.

His father frowned. "What man?"

"The man behind the grapevines. He said something about joining them? What does that mean?"

His mother clasped her hands. A scowl spread across her face.

"Is it that foolishness about a strike?" she asked.

"It's not so foolish," his father said, pounding his fist on the table. "They want us to stop picking grapes. They want us to strike for more money and better working conditions."

Luis never saw his father so heated about something. "Are we going to do it?" Luis asked.

"I don't think we should," said his sister, Carmelita.

"What do you know?" asked Luis, glaring at his sister.

"Don't fight, children," said their mother. "Your father and I will talk about this. It's time for you to go to bed."

Luis fell asleep listening to his mother and father talk. It seemed to him that they might talk throughout the night. He wasn't exactly sure what a strike was, but he knew the men were trying to change things. He also knew that he didn't like working on the farm the way things were. It would be better if they had clean water to drink.

He hated to hear his parents disagree, but he trusted that his father would make the right decision for the family. The next morning, everyone was quiet as they left the shack.

When they reached the fields, they saw people standing at the edge holding up signs. The signs read: "Better Pay" and "Clean Water." Tonio, who had talked with Luis's father, was in front. Luis stared at the people and then looked at his father. He wondered what his father would have their family do. Would they stay in the fields and pick grapes? Or would they stand on the side with the others and ask for clean water and better pay?

"Tomas, are you going to join us?" Tonio asked.

"No," said Carmelita.

Her father turned to her and said, "I'm not going to turn down a chance for you and Luis to have a better life than your mother and I have had." He grabbed Tonio's hand and said, "I'll take a sign."

Luis, his sister, and their mother joined their father at the edge of the field. Luis was happy that his father had made this choice. *Maybe things will get better*, he thought.

That day Luis and his family walked back and forth with their signs. They didn't pick grapes or work in the fields at all. They watched other men and their families arriving on trucks.

"Scabs!" the strikers called to them. Scabs are workers who don't honor a strike. They go into the fields to work, instead. Luis knew that his father had made a hard choice by joining the strike. He also knew that others might be afraid to make the same choice. He hoped that the people in the fields would see their family and then decide to join them.

When they went back to the shack after the day's strike, the owner of the fields came to see them.

"I pay you to work. If you are not working, you will have to leave. You can't live here," he said.

Luis and his family had no choice. They would have to pack and leave. They would stay that night at a friend of Tonio's.

"What do you want, anyway?" the owner called after them.

Luis turned back. He walked right up to the owner and looked him straight in the eyes. Luis stood tall. He was not afraid to say how his family felt. "We want better pay. We want a better place to live. And we want clean water. That is not much to ask."

"See if you get it," the owner said. "There are plenty of other people who will take your place in the fields."

"Not after we talk to them and ask them to join us," Luis said. "It may take time, but we will win this fight."

Luis walked away with his father's arm around him. Tomas was proud that his son wanted to fight for a better life. He had made the right choice for his family. Even Carmelita, who was scared of the strike at first, was proud of her father's choice.

As Luis and his family left the farm, they knew there were going to be hard times ahead. They knew that life would not be easy. They also knew that they were ready to join with others to fight for what was right.

The Grape Pickers' Strike

In 1965, many grape pickers in California went on strike. At that time, there were 500,000 farm workers in the state. Most were being paid 90 cents an hour to work. The work conditions were bad. There was no clean water in the fields. Farm owners sprayed dangerous pesticides on the fields while people worked. Farm workers got sick.

A man named César Chávez decided that the workers needed a union. A union is an organization that works to improve conditions and pay for workers. Chávez tried many ideas to get the grape owners to deal with his new union, the United Farm Workers. He and the workers marched, they asked people not to buy grapes, and they stopped eating. Finally, in 1970, the vineyard owners agreed to a contract with the union. The workers had won!